THE
ROADBUILDERS

BY
JAMES E. KELLY
AND
WILLIAM R. PARK

DRAWINGS BY
JOEL SNYDER

THE
ROAD

▲ ADDISON-WESLEY

BUILDERS

An Addisonian Press Book

Text Copyright © 1973 by James E. Kelly and William R. Park
Illustrations Copyright © 1973 by Joel Snyder
All Rights Reserved
Addison-Wesley Publishing Company, Inc.
Reading, Massachusetts 01867
Printed in the United States of America

Second Printing

BB/BP   05728   12/73

Library of Congress Cataloging in Publication Data
Kelly, James E.
   The roadbuilders.
   SUMMARY: Traces each step in the design and
construction of a highway and describes the machinery
used.
   "An Addisonian Press book."
   1. Road construction—Juvenile literature.
2. Road machinery—Juvenile literature. [1. Road
construction. 2. Road machinery] I. Park, William R.,
joint author. II. Snyder, Joel, illus. III. Title.
TE149.K44   625.7   72-4763
ISBN 0-201-05728-X

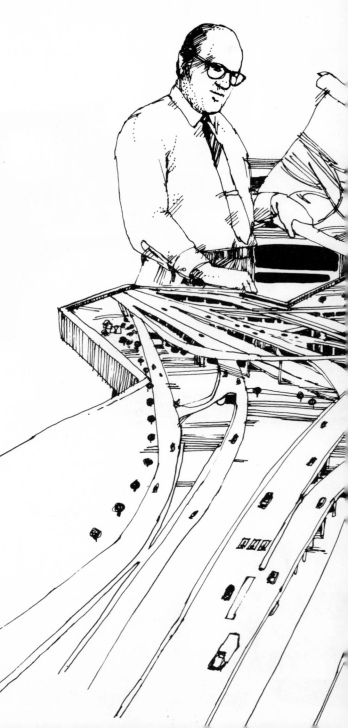

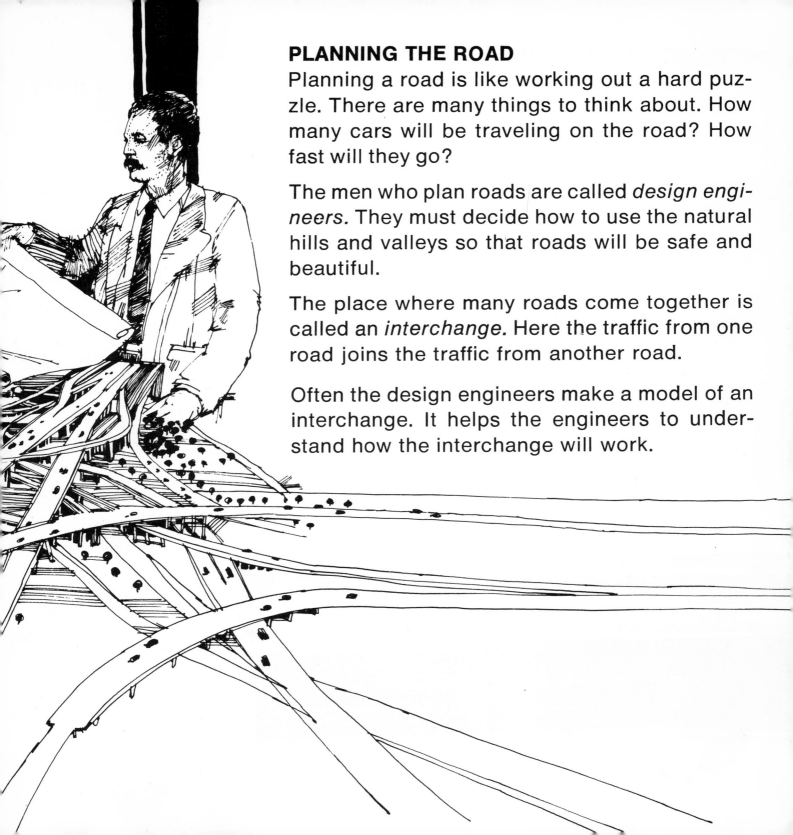

PLANNING THE ROAD

Planning a road is like working out a hard puzzle. There are many things to think about. How many cars will be traveling on the road? How fast will they go?

The men who plan roads are called *design engineers.* They must decide how to use the natural hills and valleys so that roads will be safe and beautiful.

The place where many roads come together is called an *interchange.* Here the traffic from one road joins the traffic from another road.

Often the design engineers make a model of an interchange. It helps the engineers to understand how the interchange will work.

ENGINEERS STUDY THE LAND

It takes engineers with special training to help finish plans for a road. Usually an *aerial mapper* flies over the land where the road will go. He takes photographs of the land with a *stereoscopic camera.* These pictures let the engineers measure high and low places. They can tell how high the hills are, how low the valleys are, and how wide they are.

Next, special instruments called *stereoplotters* are used to study the pictures. With a stereoplotter, an engineer can measure a bump on the ground no bigger than a stair step.

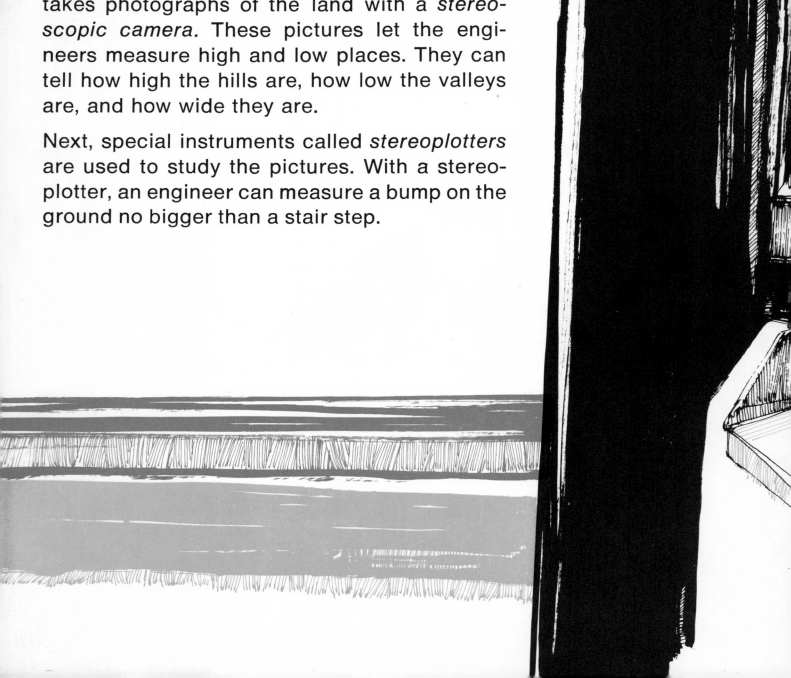

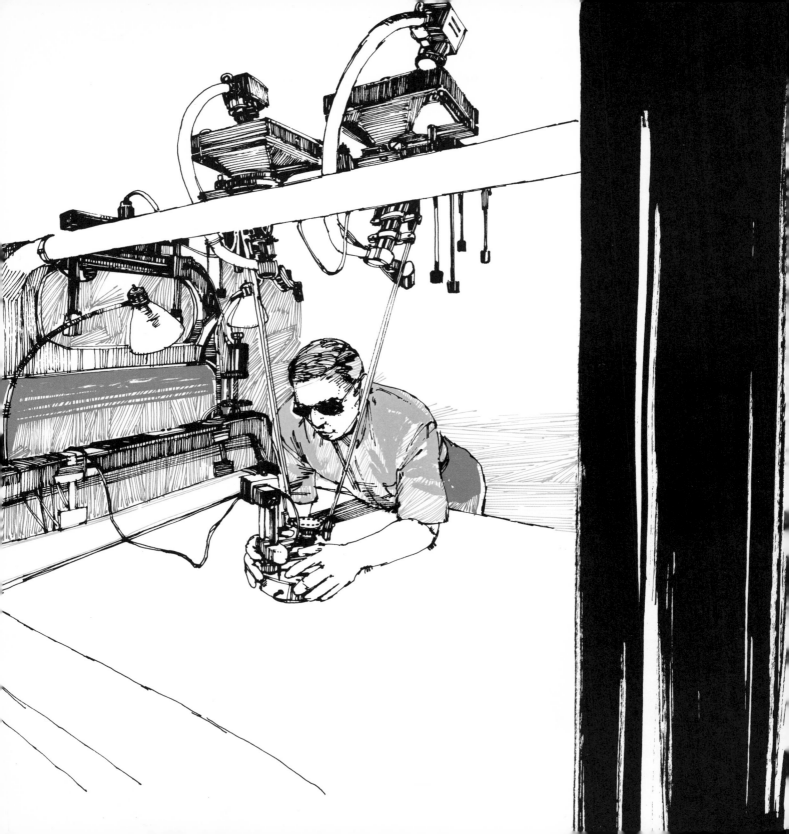

PROJECT ENGINEERS AT WORK

A *project engineer* works with the roadbuilders.
He uses the plans made by the design engineer.
The plans show him where to build the road.

The project engineer helps the roadbuilders to
use the plans. He also checks to see that the
work is done the way the plans show it should
be done.

MEN AND MACHINES

When the plans are finished it is time, for the *contractor* to begin work. The contractor hires the men and the big machines that build the roads. Some contractors own their own machines.

How is a contractor chosen to build a road? Many contractors may wish to build the road. Each contractor writes on a piece of paper the amount of money he would charge for doing the job. This amount is called a *bid*. The contractor puts his bid into an envelope and drops it into a box with all of the bids from the other contractors.

When the time comes to look at the bids, everyone is very excited, because the contractor whose bid is the lowest will get the job. Who will it be?

CLEARING THE WAY FOR THE ROAD

The contractor must first clear the land where the road will be. Clearing gets started with the crashing of brush and trees and the roar of engines. Huge tractors with special steel blades push through the brush and trees.

Some of the tractors have *brush cabs* that look like steel cages. These brush cabs protect the tractor driver from falling trees and branches.

Trees and brush are pushed into huge piles by other tractors equipped with *brush rakes.* The piles are then pushed into big holes and covered with dirt or are hauled away in trucks. When buildings are in the way, they too are cleared away.

MOVING THE EARTH FOR THE ROAD
Here they come!

Suddenly there are many machines instead of just a few. They swarm over the roadway with their engines roaring.

Some, like the *scrapers,* move as fast as galloping horses. They seem to be going in all directions, pushing dirt here and dumping it there. But each has an important job to do. Every machine operator knows exactly where he is supposed to go and what he is supposed to do.

THE BULLDOZER

A crawler tractor has many uses. When a blade is fastened on its front, it is called a bulldozer. A bulldozer pushes dirt from one place to another.

Instead of wheels with rubber tires, the crawler tractor moves along on moving steel tracks. It is not very fast but it is very powerful.

MOTOR SCRAPERS

Sometimes the road must cross steep hills and ridges and go through deep valleys. Huge earth-moving machines called *scrapers* scrape the dirt from the hills and high places and move it to the low places.

As the scraper moves, a heavy blade drops down and scoops a layer of dirt from the ground. This dirt goes up into the back end of the scraper. When it is full the scraper hauls the dirt away.

CUTS AND FILLS

The place from where the dirt is scraped away is called the *cut*, because the roadway is cut right through the hill.

The place where the dirt is dumped is called the *fill,* because the dirt is used to fill in the low spots.

After the high places are cut off and the low places are filled in, the ground will be more level. Then there will be no steep hills for the cars to climb after the road is built.

WORKING IN THE FILL

If a fill is a big one, many scrapers are used to haul and dump loads of dirt into it.

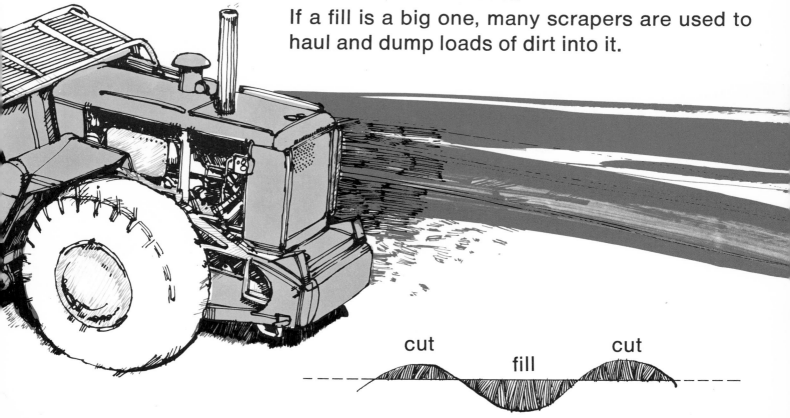

cut   fill   cut

MOTOR GRADER

The *motor grader* is an important machine to the roadbuilder. It smooths out the ground for the scrapers and spreads the dirt evenly in the fill. Now the roadway will be level. It also has other jobs, as you will soon learn.

FRONT-END LOADERS AND OFF-HIGHWAY TRUCKS

Much of the earthmoving has already been done when the cuts and fills have been leveled. But there is still a lot to do. Some of the dirt needs to be hauled away by big *off-highway trucks.* They are called this because they are too big and heavy to drive on regular highways.

The dirt is loaded into them by a tractor with a big bucket on its front end, called a *front-end loader*. The bucket picks up the dirt and dumps it into the big truck.

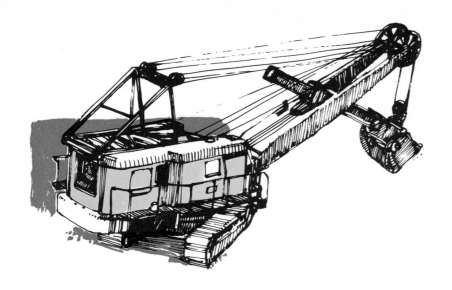

POWER SHOVELS AND HAULERS

The off-highway trucks are often loaded by a *power shovel.* The power shovel is a giant machine with one long arm. This arm is called a *boom.* The boom can move up and down, and the whole machine can swing from side to side.

On the end of the boom, a bucket with steel teeth bites off big chunks of dirt and rock and swings it over to the waiting truck.

THE CLAMSHELL

Special digging jobs where dirt has to be moved only a short distance are often done by a crane with a *clamshell* bucket. The clamshell has two parts that are hooked together and work like giant steel jaws. The clamshell drops down on the dirt, then the jaws come together and bite the earth like a big steel mouth.

WHEEL DIGGER

A giant monster called a *wheel digger* is also an earthmover. It looks like an old-fashioned riverboat with its side-wheel churning up the earth.

The wheel digs up the brown earth and dumps it onto a *conveyor belt*. The belt shoots the dirt in a steady stream into the big wagons that move along beside it.

These wagons are called bottom dumps because their bottoms have two gates which open to let the dirt out. Because of the gates it is very easy for them to dump their loads in the fill.

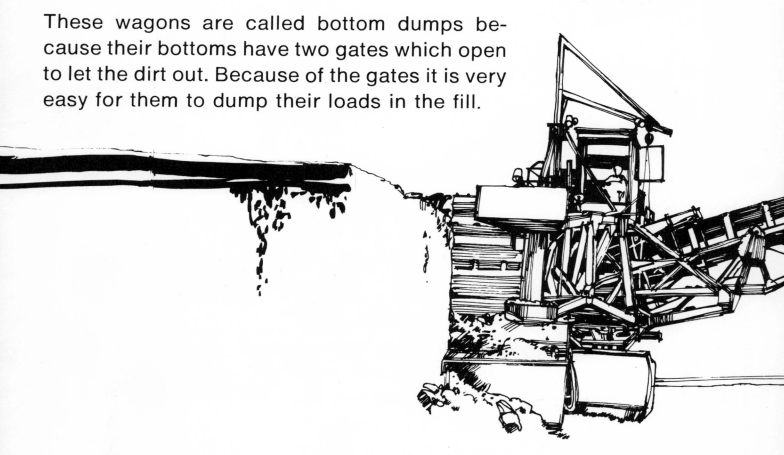

THE FLAGMAN

Watch the *flagman!*

The flagman uses a red flag or a sign with the words STOP on one side and SLOW on the other. He directs the traffic in places where cars pass through or near the job site.

You wouldn't want a big *compactor* to run over your car. Some of them are so big and heavy they would smash your car flat!

COMPACTORS

As the dirt is being placed on the fill, it must be packed down so that the ground is very hard and flat. Heavy rollers called *compactors* are moved back and forth across the loose dirt. This makes the ground hard enough to support the heavy traffic that will someday run over it.

Some compactors have rollers like big steel drums, and others have rows of steel knobs that push down into the ground. These are called *sheepsfoot rollers.*

Some compactors are pulled behind tractors. Others have their own power and look like tractors with rollers instead of wheels.

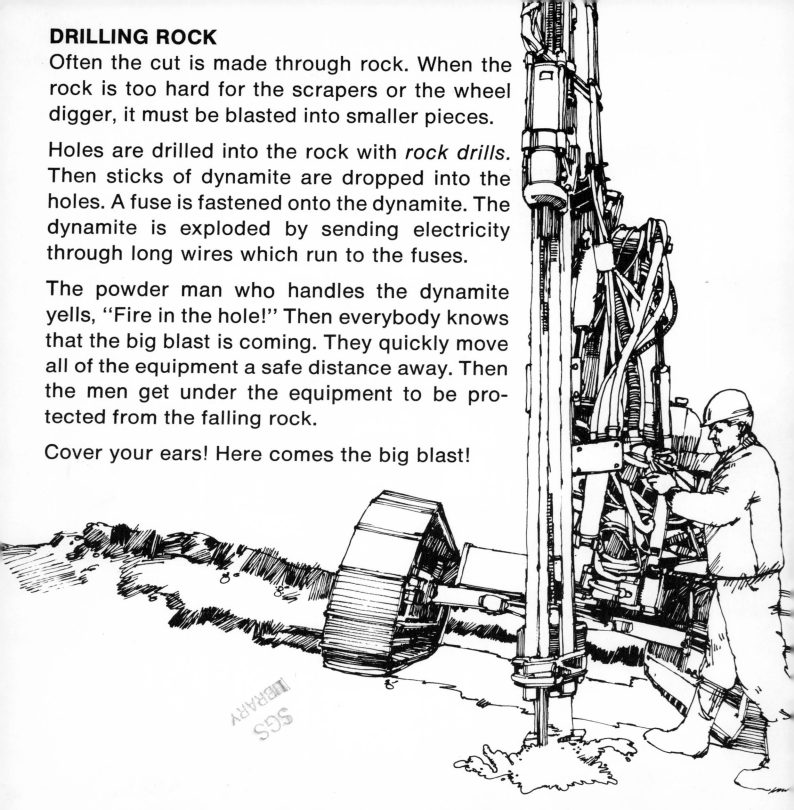

DRILLING ROCK

Often the cut is made through rock. When the rock is too hard for the scrapers or the wheel digger, it must be blasted into smaller pieces.

Holes are drilled into the rock with *rock drills.* Then sticks of dynamite are dropped into the holes. A fuse is fastened onto the dynamite. The dynamite is exploded by sending electricity through long wires which run to the fuses.

The powder man who handles the dynamite yells, "Fire in the hole!" Then everybody knows that the big blast is coming. They quickly move all of the equipment a safe distance away. Then the men get under the equipment to be protected from the falling rock.

Cover your ears! Here comes the big blast!

BLASTING ROCK

Boom!

Dirt and rocks fly into the air and the earth shakes. The explosion rips a huge hole in the solid rock and breaks it into smaller pieces. These will be scooped up, put into trucks, and hauled away. Later this rock can be crushed and used to help pave the road.

HAULING THE SHOT ROCK

After the rock has been blasted, it is called *shot rock.* It is now ready to be hauled to the rock crusher where it will be crushed into gravel.

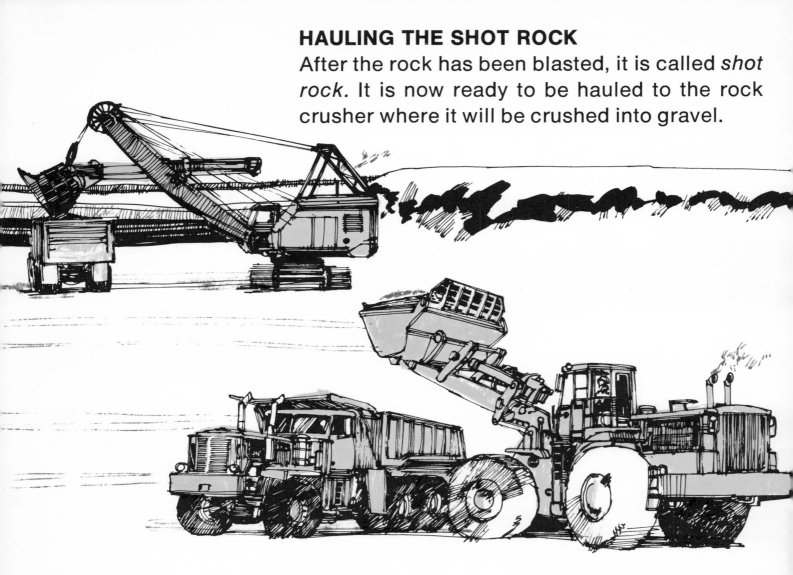

POWER SHOVELS AND LOADERS

Power shovels and front-end *loaders* handle and load the shot rock.

To break up thin layers of rock, a tractor has *ripper teeth* mounted on the back.

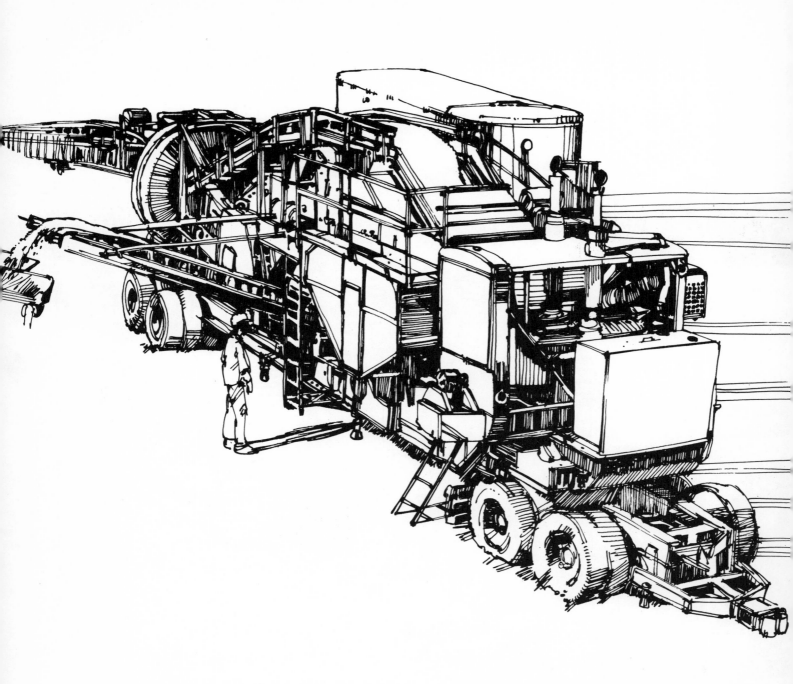

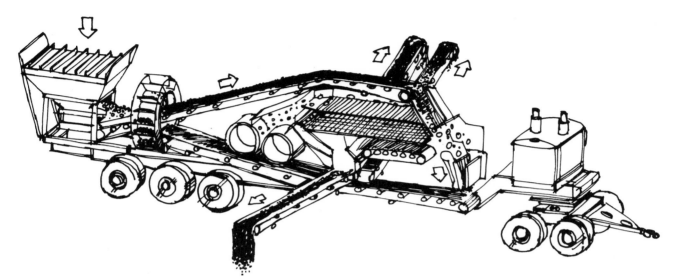

ROCK CRUSHERS

Rock crushers jiggle, shake, rattle, clatter and clang. They are the noisiest machines of all of the roadbuilders, and no wonder! They break rock into little pieces.

The shot rock is first dumped into the *primary crusher,* which breaks up the large rocks. It also sifts the rocks through screens separating the larger ones from the smaller ones.

Some of the rocks still need to be crushed into smaller pieces. They are run through a *secondary crusher* which breaks the rocks up even more and separates them into different sizes.

FINE GRADER

Soon the crushed rock will be placed on the roadbed. But before it is, the roadbed must be smoothed out by a *fine grader.* This machine moves along slowly on crawler tracks. Whirling blades under the machine cut away the bumps and high places left by the scrapers.

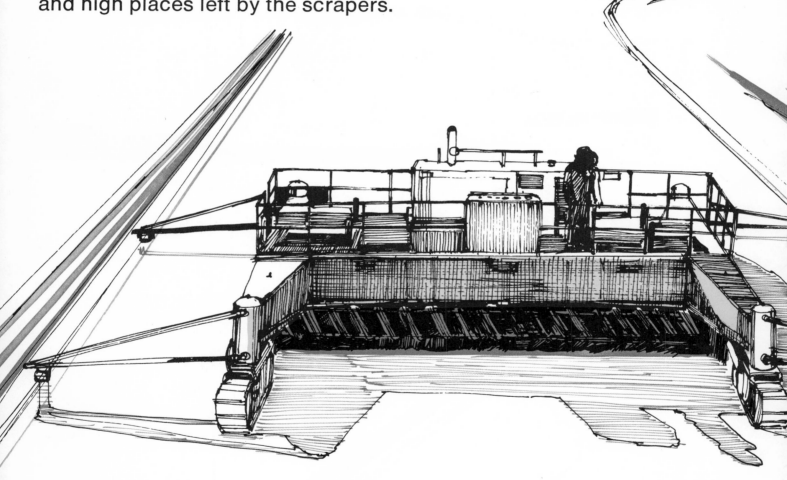

BASE ROCK

Now the gravel is dumped onto the roadbed and spread very evenly by the *rock spreader.* This gravel, called *base rock,* is then rolled by another compactor.

It has been many months since work started on the road. At last it is ready to be paved.

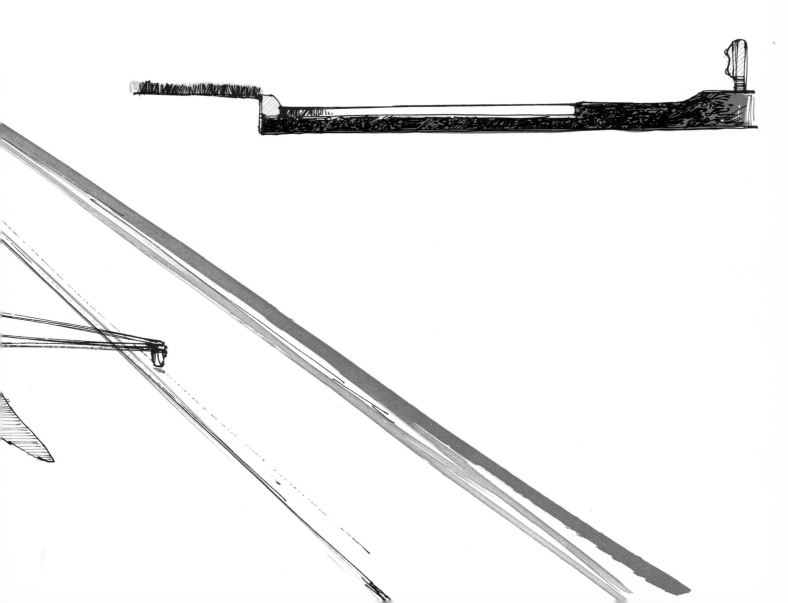

THE CENTRAL MIXING PLANT

The road may be paved with concrete which is prepared in a *central mixing plant.* It is like a small factory set up beside the highway. One mountain of stone and one of sand are waiting to be fed into the plant by conveyor belts. The stone and sand will be mixed with cement and water to make *concrete.* This will be hauled to the paving train by quick-dump trucks.

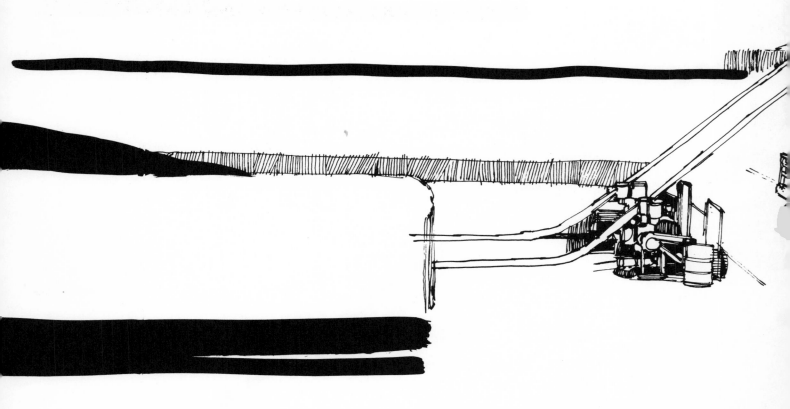

CONCRETE PAVING

Down the roadway comes the *paving train.* It is called a train because there are many machines clanking along together. Sometimes the train is pulled along on tracks like railroad tracks.

Concrete trucks hurry up to the front of the train, plopping the concrete down for the spreader to gobble up and spread into a long gray ribbon.

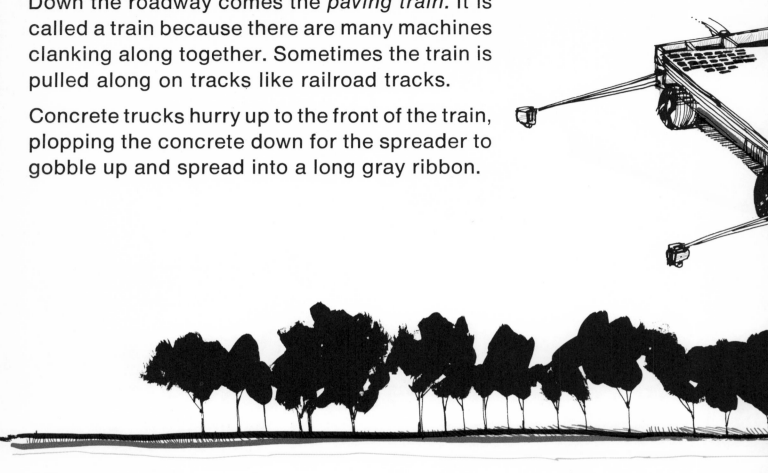

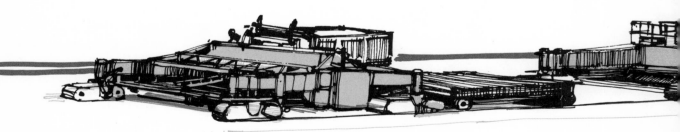

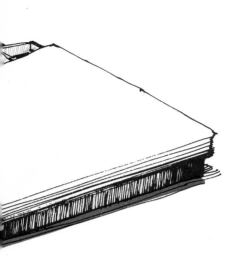

Wire mat is pressed into the wet concrete which now looks like thick gray mud. Then, before it dries and becomes hard as stone, other machines smooth the surface that the cars will drive on.

Like a big parade the paving train moves slowly along the roadway. Instead of music there is the roar of engines and the shouts of the men as they work.

Following the *spreader* and *wire mesh cart* in the parade is the *float machine.* It smooths out any bumps in the pavement surface. This machine sometimes acts like a big iron, pressing out the high and low places.

The last machine in the parade is the *finisher float*. It drags a big piece of burlap behind it. The burlap makes the surface rough to keep the cars from skidding on it.

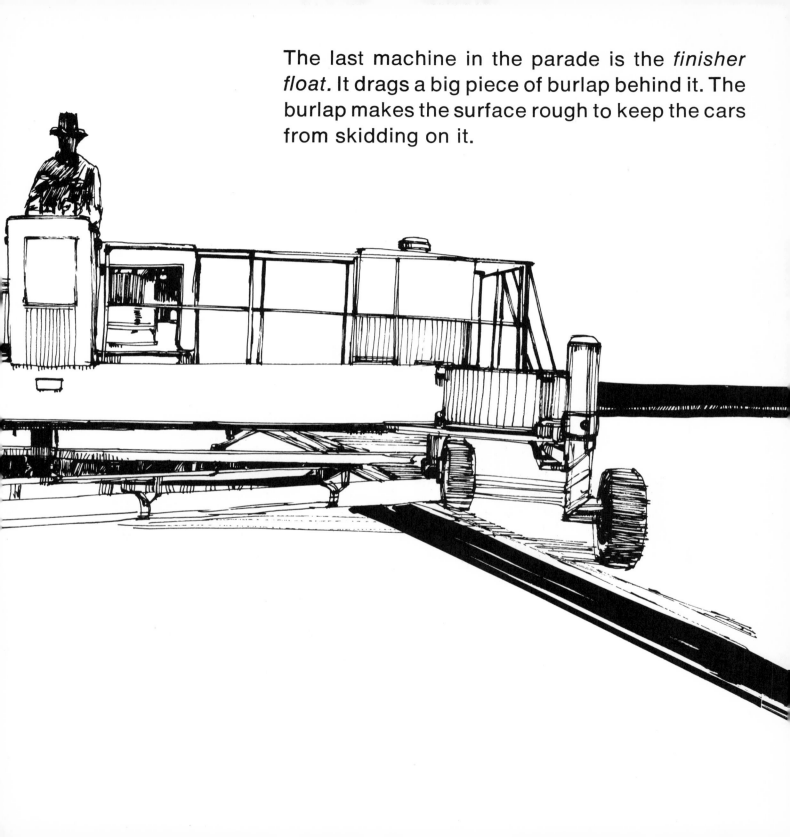

ASPHALT PAVING

Look, a black road! This is a different type of surface, called *asphalt,* or *black-top.* There is no long paving train here, only funny little *asphalt paving machines.* The dump trucks back up to the pavers with their load of hot asphalt. The pavers spread layer after layer of the asphalt until the pavement is as thick as the engineers want it.

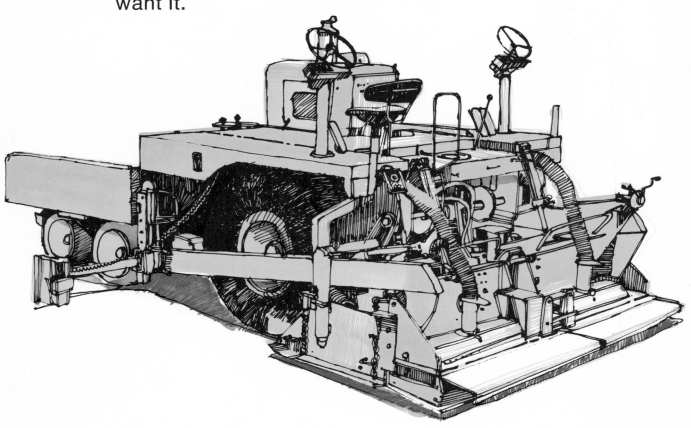

THE ASPHALT PLANT

The first thing you notice about an asphalt plant is that it is very hot. The hottest place is the *drier,* which looks like a big turning tube. It works like a clothes drier, but it is much larger and many, many times hotter.

Shooting down the middle of the drier's tube is a scorching flame that roars so loudly it can be heard a block away.

Aggregate (crushed rock) is fed into the drier from the *cold feed bins* while it is still hot. Then it is mixed with *mineral filler* (powdered rock) and *hot asphalt.*

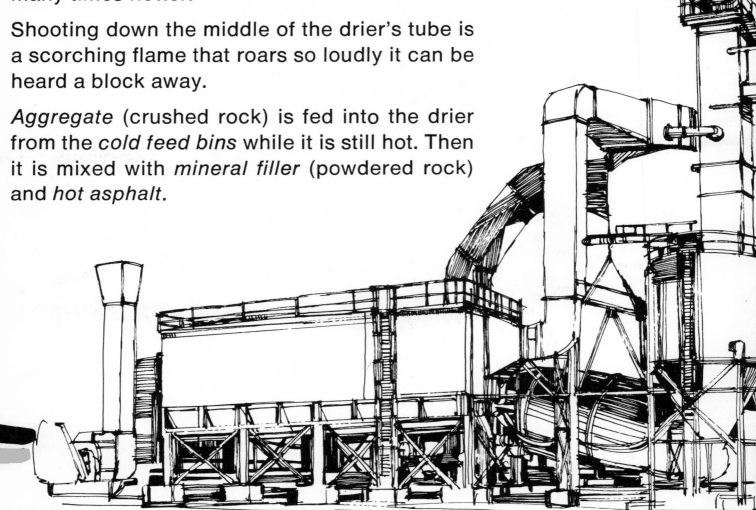

CONTROL ROOM

Because the asphalt plant is so hot, it is operated from an air-conditioned *control room.* The inside of the control room is like a spaceship; there are many buttons, dials, and knobs.

ASPHALT COMPACTORS

After the asphalt is spread by the pavers, it is rolled by compactors while it is still hot. The compactors have both steel drum and rubber-tired rollers. They pack down the black pavement to make it hard and smooth.

FINISH GRADING

Even after the road is paved there is still work to be done. The side of the road is smoothed out by *motor graders* and other special machines.

Later, grass, shrubs, and flowers will be planted along the roadway to make it beautiful.

At the same time, work on the *overpass* is going on.

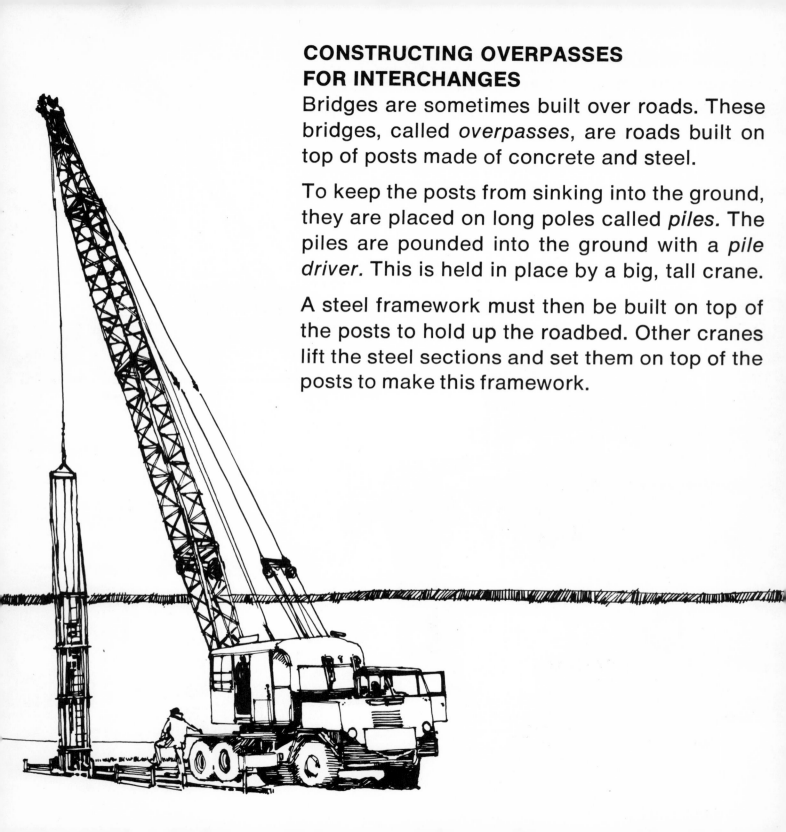

CONSTRUCTING OVERPASSES FOR INTERCHANGES

Bridges are sometimes built over roads. These bridges, called *overpasses*, are roads built on top of posts made of concrete and steel.

To keep the posts from sinking into the ground, they are placed on long poles called *piles.* The piles are pounded into the ground with a *pile driver.* This is held in place by a big, tall crane.

A steel framework must then be built on top of the posts to hold up the roadbed. Other cranes lift the steel sections and set them on top of the posts to make this framework.

PAVING THE OVERPASS

The overpass must be paved with concrete. First concrete forms which are like big wooden boxes are built to hold the concrete. Then the concrete is poured into special buckets that are lifted into place by a crane. The buckets have small doors at the bottom which open to let the concrete pour out in the right place.

After the concrete has dried, it becomes very hard. The wooden forms can then be taken away.

THE ROAD—SAFE AND BEAUTIFUL

Now everything has been done to make the road safe and beautiful. Signs are put up which tell directions, speed limits, when to stop and where to drive. Grass, shrubbery, and flowers are planted on the roadside to add to the beauty of the road.

At last the road is built. After months of hard work, the road is ready for the trucks and their loads of goods. It is ready for the cars and buses that will bring people together in the cities or take them out to the country.

About the Authors

The authors of THE ROADBUILDERS are two very active men in the construction industry. And with the help of their wives—both experienced teachers—their expertise was directed to the young reader.

James E. Kelly is the educational director of the Heavy Constructors Association of Greater Kansas City, a chapter of the Associated General Contractors of America.

Besides following major national construction projects, he also has an interest in government, currently serving as president of the Kansas City International Relations Council to study foreign affairs; he was formerly mayor pro-tem of Independence, Missouri, where he and his wife now live.

William R. Park is now principal construction economist at Midwest Research Institute. He is a licensed professional engineer, active in the American Society of Civil Engineers and other technical and professional organizations.

His many articles have appeared in a variety of construction journals. Mr. Park and his family live in Prairie Village, Kansas.

About the Artist

Joel Snyder has illustrated several children's books since graduating from the Rhode Island School of Design.

Mr. Snyder, his wife and twin boys live in Farmingville, New York where they enjoy camping and golfing.